CHINESE COOKBOOK FOR BEGINNERS

Restaurant Favorites and Authentic Chinese Recipes

(Chinese Cookbook for Delightful Home Cooking)

Willie Willer

Published by Sharon Lohan

© Willie Willer

All Rights Reserved

Chinese Cookbook for Beginners: Restaurant Favorites and Authentic Chinese Recipes (Chinese Cookbook for Delightful Home Cooking)

ISBN 978-1-990334-30-6

All rights reserved. No part of this guide may be reproduced in any form without permission in writing from the publisher except in the case of brief quotations embodied in critical articles or reviews.

Legal & Disclaimer

The information contained in this book is not designed to replace or take the place of any form of medicine or professional medical advice. The information in this book has been provided for educational and entertainment purposes only.

The information contained in this book has been compiled from sources deemed reliable, and it is accurate to the best of the Author's knowledge; however, the Author cannot guarantee its accuracy and validity and cannot be held liable for any errors or omissions. Changes are periodically made to this book. You must consult your doctor or get professional medical advice before using any of the suggested remedies, techniques, or information in this book.

Table of contents

Part 1 1
Recipe 1: Chow Mein 2
Recipe 2: Chicken Wings the Chinese way 4
Recipe 3: Chicken with Vegetables and Rice 5
Recipe 4: Chinese Vege Burgers 7
Recipe 5: Chicken with Sesame 9
Recipe 6: Cabbage and Cheese Rolls 11
Recipe 7: Chicken with Champignons........................ 13
Recipe 8: Pork on Chinese Way 15
Recipe 9: Chicken with Peanuts 17
Recipe 10: Baozi.. 19
Recipe 11: Chinese Spaghetti..................................... 21
Recipe 12: Beef Meat with Onion 23
Recipe 13: Chicken with Zucchini 25
Recipe 14: Chicken with Green Beans 27
Recipe 15: Rice with Leek... 29
Recipe 16: Chinese Steak 31
Recipe 17: Broccoli with Garlic................................... 33
Recipe 18: Chicken with Vegetables and Peanuts 35
Recipe 19: Beef from Sichuan 37

Recipe 20: Summer Meal 39

Recipe 21: Spinach with Sesame and Ginger 41

Recipe 22: Meat and Vegetables with Sweet/Sour Sauce 43

Recipe 23: Pork Meat with Champignons and Eggs 46

Recipe 24: Jiaozi 48

Recipe 25: Chicken with Honey 50

Recipe 26: Spicy Vegetables 52

Recipe 27: "Mame" 54

Recipe 28: Spicy Eggplants 56

Recipe 29: Three colors meal 58

Recipe 30: Chicken with Celery 60

Part 2 62

Introduction 63

Vegan "Egg" Drop Soup 64

Vegan Hot and Sour Soup 65

Chinese "Chicken" Salad 67

Steamed Dumplings 69

Vegan Fried Rice 71

Ginger Teriyaki Noodles 72

Vegan Chinese Noodles 74

Chinese Pear and Avocado Bowl 76

Spicy Sesame Peanut Noodles 77

- Vegetable Lo Mein 78
- Eggplant and Potato Chinese Dish............................... 80
- Vegan Orange Chicken 82
- Kung Pao "Chicken" & Vegetables 83
- "Chicken" and Broccoli.. 85
- "Beef" and Broccoli Stir Fry... 87
- Chicken and Mushroom Stir Fry 89
- Vegan Sweet and Sour "Chicken"............................... 91
- 8 TREASURE RICE PUDDING 94
- Vegan Almond Cookies 96
- Chinese lunch Recipes... 97
- Chinese Fried Rice.. 97
- Chinese Roasted Chicken 100
- Chinese Chicken with Black Pepper Sauce 102
- Chinese Beef With Broccoli.. 104
- Chinese Grilled Chicken 107
- Chinese Spicy Beef Lettuce Wraps 109
- Ground Beef Chinese Style... 111
- Chinese Sesame Limas 113
- Chinese Spaghetti 115
- Chinese Chicken Manchurian..................................... 117
- Chinese Dinner Recipes... 119

Beefy Chinese Dumplings 119

Chinese Scallion Pancakes 121

Crab Rangoon 123

Pumpkin Bread Recipe 125

Lighter Chicken Egg Foo Young 127

Quick Chinese-Style Vermicelli 129

Stir-Fried Cabbage 131

Chinese Broccoli 133

Easy Fried Spinach 135

Chinese Soup Recipes 136

Chinese Lion's Head Soup 136

Chinese Sizzling Rice Soup 139

Chinese Chicken Soup 141

Chinese Corn Soup 143

Chinese Egg Soup 145

Quick Veggie Soup 146

Egg Drop Soup 148

Homemade Wonton Soup 150

Asian-Style Chicken Noodle Soup 153

Hot and Sour Soup with Tofu 155

Chinese Salad Recipes 157

Asian Chicken Salad 157

Conclusion 159

Part 1

Recipe 1: Chow Mein

Chicken with pasta. Really easy and fast to make!

Total Prep Time: **20 minutes**

Yield: 4

List of Ingredients:

- 14 oz. of pasta
- 17 oz. of chicken meat
- 1 red bell pepper
- 1 zucchini
- 1 garlic
- 7 oz. of peas
- 1 chilli pepper
- 3 tablespoons of soya sauce
- 3 tablespoons of olive oil
- 1 tablespoon of flour
- Salt and pepper to taste
- 1 tablespoon of sesame oil

Methods:

1. Cut pepper, chili, onion, zucchini, garlic and meat into small pieces. (Lines or circles)

2. Spice the chicken with soya sauce, sesame oil, salt and pepper.

3. Prepare the meat in a frying pan. (3 to 4 minutes only)

4. Add pepper, zucchini and peas. Fry for 3 to 4 more minutes.

5. Cook the pasta in a cooking pot, with salt water.

6. Add pasta into the frying pan and stir fry for 1 more minute.

7. There you go, fast and easy!

Recipe 2: Chicken Wings the Chinese way

Total Prep Time: **35 minutes**

Yield: 4

List of Ingredients:

- 28 oz. of chicken wings
- 2 cups of oil
- 1 cup of soya sauce
- ½ cup of cognac
- 2 tablespoons of salt
- 2 tablespoons of pepper

Methods:

1. Mix soya sauce, cognac, salt and pepper in one bowl.

2. Soak the wings into the mixture and let it sit there for around 2 hours.

3. After that, fry the wings in hot oil.

4. Serve it hot, with rice!

Recipe 3: Chicken with Vegetables and Rice

This is one of the most famous Chinese meals. Probably everyone knows about this one, and everyone at least has tried this at a local Chinese Fast Food restaurant. It is very fast and easy to make!

Total Prep Time: **20 minutes**

Yield: 4

List of Ingredients:

- 1 pack of mixed Chinese vegetables
- 14 oz. of chicken breasts
- ½ cup of rice
- Pinch of salt and pepper
- Curry and soy sauce to taste
- 1 onion

Methods:

1. Cut chicken breasts into small rectangular pieces. Add curry and salt.

2. Cut the onion and fry it for 2 minutes. Then, add the chicken and fry for 3 more minutes.

3. Remove the meat from the frying pan and add vegetable mix. Fry for 10 more minutes while stirring constantly.

4. While vegetables are frying, cook the rice:

a. Wash rice and put it in a cooking pot with 2 cups of water.

b. Add salt to taste and cook for around 15 minutes.

5. In the end, mix everything together. Add soy sauce and pepper to taste.

6. Serve hot and enjoy!

Recipe 4: Chinese Vege Burgers

Total Prep Time: **35 minutes**

Yield: 3

List of Ingredients:

- 1 zucchini
- 1 onion
- 1 pack of Chinese vegetable mix
- 2 tablespoons of soya sauce
- 2 tablespoons of chili sauce
- 1 tablespoon of ginger (powdered)
- ½ cup of yogurt
- 6 kaiser rolls
- 1 leek

Methods:

1. Peel the zucchini and cut it into small circles. Pour them with chili and bake for 10 minutes at 300°F.

2. Cut onion and fry it for a few minutes.

3. Add vegetable mix to the frying pan. Stir for a while and then add soya sauce and other spices. Let it fry for 15 minutes. (Add water if needed)

4. Prepare the sauce:

a. Mix yogurt, 1 tablespoons of soya sauce, 1 tablespoon of chilli

5. Cut kaiser rolls in half, spread the sauce on both sides. Add vegetables.

6. Enjoy this healthy meal!

Recipe 5: Chicken with Sesame

Sesame is now widely used in the everyday kitchen. It is used in a lot of meals because of its delicious flavor it gives to every meal (savory or sweet). Did you know that Sesame has been used in Chinese cuisine for centuries?

Total Prep Time: **40 minutes**

Yield: 5

List of Ingredients:

- 28 oz. of chicken breast (in fillets)
- 1 lemon juice
- 2 tablespoons of soya sauce
- 1 tablespoon of pepper
- 1 tablespoon of salt
- 4 tablespoons of oil

For panning:

- 3 tablespoons of flour
- 3 eggs
- Pinch of salt

- 1 tablespoon of pepper
- 12 oz. of sesame
- 2 tablespoons of breadcrumbs

Methods:

1. Cut the meat into bigger pieces. Pour lemon juice, salt, pepper and soya sauce on the meat. Let it sit for a while.

2. Beat the eggs, and spice them with a pinch of salt and 1 tablespoon of pepper.

3. Roll meat pieces into flour and then in the egg mixture.

4. Now, pour sesame onto them. (Or roll the meat into sesame)

5. Fry meat pieces in a frying pan.

6. Serve hot or cold and enjoy!

Recipe 6: Cabbage and Cheese Rolls

Total Prep Time: **30 minutes**

Yield: 4

List of Ingredients:

- 8 oz. of puff pastry
- ½ cabbage head
- 1 carrot
- 1 onion
- 1 tablespoon of soya sauce
- 4 oz. of cheese (any)
- 3 tablespoons of oil
- Spices to taste

Methods:

1. Cut cabbage, carrot, and onion into small lines. Fry them in a frying pan for close to 15 minutes. Add spices (pepper, ginger, chili and soya sauce).

2. Knead the puff pastry. Spread the vegetables and cheese over it.

3. Roll the dough and cut them into any size you like.

4. Place them into a casserole dish for 20 minutes at 300°F and bake.

Recipe 7: Chicken with Champignons

Again, very easy to make which is mostly a key feature of Chinese cuisine!

Total Prep Time: **40 minutes**

Yield: 4

List of Ingredients:

- 14. oz. of chicken meat
- 7 oz. of champignons
- 1 tablespoon of oil
- 1 garlic
- 1 tablespoon of cut ginger
- Salt and pepper to taste
- ½ tablespoon of sesame oil (optional)

Methods:

1. Cut the meat into small pieces. Cut champignons into thick lines.

2. Fry meat in the hot oil, remove it from the frying pan. Put the champignons into the same frying pan.

3. Cut garlic and ginger into small pieces.

4. After a few minutes, mix everything together (meat, champignons, ginger, garlic, salt and pepper).

5. Serve with rice or any salad!

Recipe 8: Pork on Chinese Way

Total Prep Time: **20 minutes**

Yield: 2

List of Ingredients:

- 7 oz. of pork meat
- 7 oz. of champignons
- 1 cup of wine
- 2 tablespoons of soya sauce
- 1 tablespoon of curry sauce
- Salt and pepper to taste
- 7 oz. of pasta

Methods:

1. Cut meat into small lines or cubes. Soak it in the soya sauce and let it sit for 30 minutes.

2. Fry the meat in a frying pan with oil. Add champignons.

3. After some few minutes, add wine and curry sauce.

4. Cook the pasta in a cooking pot. When it is done, add it to the frying pan.

5. You can add parmesan on the top and serve when ready!

Recipe 9: Chicken with Peanuts

The exotic, strange but delicious combination makes this meal my personal favorite!

Total Prep Time: **60 minutes**

Yield: 2

List of Ingredients:

- 9 oz. of chicken fillets
- 4 oz. of green onion
- 4 oz. of peanuts
- 1 tablespoon of red bell pepper (cut)
- 2 tablespoons of oil
- ½ cup of soya sauce
- 2 garlics
- 1 cup of water
- ½ cup of white wine
- Salt and pepper to taste

Methods:

1. Wash chicken fillets, dry them and cut into cubes.

2. Cut the broth and garlic on the rings and wash it.

3. In heated oil, fry the peanuts briefly and then take it out with a slotted serving spoon.

4. In the same frying pan, fry meat for about 10 minutes, and then remove it with a slotted serving spoon too.

5. Fry green onion and red bell pepper in the same frying pan.

6. Return chicken and peanuts to the pan and mix them well with the green onion and pepper.

7. In one bowl, mix water, soy sauce, ginger, wine, and spices.

8. Pour the chopped chicken with this mixture and fry it all together just for a few minutes more.

9. Serve when ready.

Recipe 10: Baozi

Total Prep Time: **35 minutes**

Yield: 6

List of Ingredients:

For the dough:

- 17 oz. of flour
- 2 cups of water
- 1 pack of yeast
- Pinch of salt

For the topping:

- 8 oz. of meat (any)
- 1 egg
- 2 tablespoons of soya sauce
- 1 tablespoon of sesame oil
- Pinch of salt
- 1 tablespoon of ginger (cut or minced)
- 1 leek

- 2 tablespoons of oil

Methods:

1. Prepare the dough with given ingredient.

2. Prepare the topping:

a. Mix every ingredient listed for the topping.

3. Cut 15 small pieces of the dough.

4. Put 1 tablespoon of the topping mixture into each one.

5. Bake Baozi for 15 minutes on steam. You can use bamboo pot.

6. Serve when ready.

Recipe 11: Chinese Spaghetti

Spaghetti is celebrated by Italian cuisine, but its fame is in fact that Marco Polo, the sailor, named Spaghetti – He fell in love with a beautiful Chinese girl who was perfectly skillful in kneading the doughs into thin threads.

Total Prep Time: **50 minutes**

Yield: 4

List of Ingredients:

- 7 oz. of thicker spaghetti
- 7 oz. of champignons
- 2 garlics
- 4 oz. of carrot
- 7 oz. of zucchini
- 3 oz. of spinach
- 4 tablespoons of oil
- 1 tablespoon of ginger
- 1 onion

- 1 tablespoon of soya sauce

Methods:

1. Peel, wash and cut the vegetables. Cut garlic and zucchini into thick lines, champignons into rings, and onion into small rectangular pieces and grate carrots.

2. Sauté carrot and garlic together with a little bit of oil.

3. Cook spaghetti in water – but not completely! Dry them and keep it warm.

4. In a heated frying pan, add oil, onion and zucchini. Sauté for few minutes.

5. In a different frying pan, sauté champignons and spinach.

6. Mix everything together and pour the resulting mixture onto the spaghetti.

7. Add ginger, soya sauce, salt and pepper to taste. Mix it and stir it for a while.

8. After 5 to 10 minutes, it should be done. You can eat the meal just like this or with chicken meal!

Recipe 12: Beef Meat with Onion

Bi Jiao, on Chinese means "eight angles" – which describes Anise. In Europe, anise is used mostly in sweet meals/desserts. But in China, it is used even with the meat!

Total Prep Time: **40 minutes**

Yield: 2

List of Ingredients:
- 7 oz. of beef
- 2 onions
- 1 cup of water
- 1 tablespoon of soya sauce
- 1 tablespoon of salt
- 1 tablespoon of pepper
- 1 anise
- 2 tablespoons of oil
- 1 tablespoon of sesame oil

Methods:

1. Cut beef into lines. Pour soya sauce over it and let it sit for 60 minutes.

2. In one bowl, mix water, salt and pepper.

3. Fry the meat in hot oil, pour it with the spices. When it is done, remove it from the frying pan.

4. Put the anise into the same frying pan, add onion (which you previously cut into small pieces). Fry them together for a few minutes.

5. Add meat again. Pour everything with the salt and pepper mix and sesame oil.

6. Serve when ready.

Recipe 13: Chicken with Zucchini

Total Prep Time: **40 minutes**

Yield: 4

List of Ingredients:

- 14 oz. of chicken meat
- 14 oz. of zucchini
- 1 cup of oil
- 1 tablespoon of salt
- 1 tablespoon of ginger
- ½ cup of water
- ½ cup of wine
- 1 tablespoon of sesame oil

Methods:

1. Cut chicken meat into lines. Cut zucchinis into halves (do not peel them) and then cut them into lines too.

2. Heat the oil in a frying pan. Put the meat and fry them for a few minutes. Add salt.

3. Remove the meat from the frying pan and add zucchini. Fry for 3 to 4 minutes. Add salt and ginger. Put the meat back in the frying pan along with the water and wine.

4. Add sesame oil and fry everything together.

5. Serve with rice!

Recipe 14: Chicken with Green Beans

Total Prep Time: **45 minutes**

Yield: 4

List of Ingredients:

- 14 oz. of green beans
- 7 oz. of tofu
- 1 garlic
- 1 tablespoon of sesame oil
- 2 tablespoons of soya sauce
- 4 oz. of corn
- 7 oz. of carrot
- 2 tablespoons of white wine
- 3 tablespoons of olive oil

Methods:

1. Clean the green beans, wash them and cook in water for 20 minutes.

2. On olive oil, fry onion, carrot and pepper (which you previously cut). After they are done, keep them in a warm place.

3. In the same oil, fry tofu, add garlic, wine, soya sauce, and sesame oil.

4. After few minutes, add fried vegetables, green beans, and corn.

5. Serve when ready.

Recipe 15: Rice with Leek

Total Prep Time: **25 minutes**

Yield: 2

List of Ingredients:

- 3.5 oz. of rice
- 10 oz. of leek
- 2 tablespoons of oil
- Spices to taste

Methods:

1. Cook the rice in hot water (without salt).

2. Clean the leek, wash it and cut into thick rings.

3. Sauté leek in a hot oil, add spices to taste and add to rice.

4. Mix everything together and sauté for a few minutes.

5. Serve when ready.

Recipe 16: Chinese Steak

Total Prep Time: **30 minutes**

Yield: 4

List of Ingredients:

- 20 oz. of beef meat
- 2 egg-whites
- 2 tablespoons of corn starch
- 1 tablespoon of soya sauce
- 1 garlic
- Salt and pepper to taste

Methods:

1. Blend the egg-white with soya sauce. Also, blend the garlic.

2. Pour the salt, pepper and blended garlic over meat.

3. Put the corn starch in one bowl, and sink the meat. Pour the egg-white/soya sauce mixture over the meat and let it sit through the night. (In a fridge)

4. Heat the oil in a frying pan. Fry the meat on both sides.

5. You can add ginger or chili pepper!

Recipe 17: Broccoli with Garlic

Total Prep Time: **30 minutes**

Yield: 2

List of Ingredients:

- 14 oz. of broccoli
- 3 garlics
- 3 tablespoons of oil
- 1 tablespoon of pepper
- 1 tablespoon of salt
- 1 cup of water
- 1 tablespoon of ginger

Methods:

1. Clean the broccoli, wash it and cut into small pieces.

2. Cook it in boiling water along with the 2 tablespoons of oil.

3. In a frying pan, add cooked broccoli, 1 tablespoon of oil, salt and pepper. Fry for 5 minutes.

4. Cut garlic into small pieces.

5. Mix water, ginger and broccoli in a bowl. Add cut garlic and mix again.

6. Cook everything just for a few minutes, and enjoy!

Recipe 18: Chicken with Vegetables and Peanuts

Total Prep Time: **60 minutes**

Yield: 6

List of Ingredients:

- 24 oz. of chicken meat
- 30 oz. of vegetable mix (carrots, peas, red bell pepper, green bell pepper, onion, bamboo, corn)
- 2 cups of soya sauce
- 1 tablespoon of ginger
- 2 tablespoons of oil
- 3 tablespoons of peanuts
- 4 tablespoons of corn starch
- 3 tablespoons of sesame oil

For the sauce:

- ½ cup of pineapple juice
- 4 tablespoons of ketchup

- 2 tablespoons of brown sugar
- 2 tablespoons of corn starch
- 2 tablespoons of soya sauce
- ½ tablespoon of milled ginger
- 3 to 4 pineapple rings

Methods:

1. Cut vegetables and meat into lines.

2. Pour the meat with 4 tablespoons of corn starch, 3 tablespoons of sesame oil, and 2 tablespoons of soya sauce.

3. Let it sit for 30 minutes.

4. In a frying pan, fry the meat first. After a few minutes, add vegetables and soya sauce and fry for another 20 minutes with constant stirring. At the end, add peanuts.

5. Prepare the sauce:

a. Mix every ingredient listed (except pineapple rings).

b. Cook until it gets dense, then add pineapple.

6. Pour the sauce over the meat/vegetables mix.

7. Serve when ready.

Recipe 19: Beef from Sichuan

Total Prep Time: **40 minutes**

Yield: 4

List of Ingredients:

- 10 oz. of beef meat
- 1 cup of oil
- 2 carrots
- 4 red bell pepper
- 1 onion
- 2 oz. of champignons
- 2 tablespoons of soya sauce
- ½ tablespoon of ginger
- 1 tablespoon of chili pepper
- ½ tablespoon of salt
- Salt and pepper to taste

Methods:

1. Cut the meat, champignons and vegetables into small lines.

2. Heat the oil in a frying pan, add beef. Fry until it gets brown.

3. Remove the meat, and add carrots, pepper and onion.

4. Cook the champignons in boiling water for 20 minutes. After that, add them to the frying pan too.

5. Mix everything together. Add soya sauce, chili pepper, and spices to taste.

6. Serve this meal with rice!

Recipe 20: Summer Meal

Chinese eat this kind of meal only during summer!

Total Prep Time: **40 minutes**

Yield: 4

List of Ingredients:

- 11 oz. of pork meat
- 4 oz. of carrot
- 2 red bell peppers
- 4 onions
- 1 tablespoon of tomato sauce
- 2 garlic
- 1 pepperoni
- 4 tablespoons of oil
- ½ cup of water
- Salt to taste
- 1 cut parsley

Methods:

1. Cut vegetables and meat into small lines.

2. Fry the meat with oil in a frying pan.

3. Add carrot, pepper, onion, garlic, pepperoni, and salt to taste. Mix constantly.

4. In the end, add tomato sauce and ½ cup of water.

5. Pour cut parsley over and serve the meal!

Recipe 21: Spinach with Sesame and Ginger

This can be a wonderful side dish for various meals!

Total Prep Time: **25 minutes**

Yield: 4

List of Ingredients:

- 14 oz. of spinach
- 1 tablespoon of sesame seeds
- 1 tablespoon of ginger
- 2 tablespoons of soya sauce
- ½ cup of water
- 2 tablespoons of oil
- 1 tablespoon of sesame oil

Methods:

1. Wash spinach and dry it.

2. Heat the oil in a frying pan. Add ginger and sesame seeds. Sauté them just for 1 minute.

3. Add spinach and sauté for 2 more minutes. Add soya sauce, water and spices to taste.

4. Stir fry for 3 more minutes and then add sesame oil.

5. Here you go!

Recipe 22: Meat and Vegetables with Sweet/Sour Sauce

Total Prep Time: **60 minutes**

Yield: 2

List of Ingredients:

- 17 oz. of chicken meat
- 1 tablespoon of chili pepper
- 1 cup of milk
- 4 oz. of rice
- 3 tablespoons of sesame
- 3 tablespoons of oil
- 1 onion
- 4 garlic
- 3 oz. of champignons
- 1 carrot
- 3.5 oz. of broccoli
- 1 red bell pepper

For the sauce:
- 1 cup of water
- 3 tablespoons of sugar
- 3 tablespoons of aceto balsamico
- 5 tablespoons of soya sauce
- 1 tablespoon of ketchup
- 2 tablespoons of corn starch

Methods:

1. Cut vegetables, meat, and champignons into small lines.

2. Sink chicken meat into milk and let it sit in a fridge for 30 minutes.

3. Then, remove it from the milk, add salt, pepper, and oil. Put it into a casserole dish and bake for 20 minutes at 300°F.

4. Cook the rice in water, with salt.

5. Heat 2 tablespoons of oil in a frying pan. Add onion and garlic – let it fry for 1 minute. Add carrot, champignons and stir for 5 more minutes.

6. Add broccoli, red and green bell peppers and stir fry for 10 more minutes. Add sesame in the end.

7. Prepare Sweet/Sour sauce:

a. Mix every ingredient listed "For the sauce", except corn starch.

b. Heat them for 3 to 4 minutes. Add corn starch (mixed with ½ cup of water). Mix until it gets dense.

8. Pour meat and rice with this sauce. Bon apetit!

Recipe 23: Pork Meat with Champignons and Eggs

Total Prep Time: **40 minutes**

Yield: 2

List of Ingredients:

- 7 oz. of pork meat
- 2 garlic
- 1 tablespoons of sugar
- 1 oz. of champignons
- 1 tablespoon of soya sauce
- 2 cups of water
- 2 eggs
- 2 tablespoons of oil
- Pinch of salt

Methods:

1. Cut the meat into lines.

2. Wash champignons and dry them. Then, cook them for a few minutes and dry again.

3. Melt the sugar in a frying pan (with oil). Add meat, mix and add 2 cups of water.

4. In a bowl, mix champignons, garlic, ginger, sesame oil and soya sauce. Cook the mixture on medium heat until it gets soft.

5. Beat the eggs, add salt and pepper. Make the scrambled eggs.

6. Serve it together with yogurt!

Recipe 24: Jiaozi

This meal is all about the joy! It is prepared by the whole family for a Chinese New Year.

Total Prep Time: **90 minutes**

Yield: 4

List of Ingredients:

For the dough:

- 17 oz. of flour
- 2 cups of water

For the topping:

- 7 oz. of minced meat
- 7 oz. of spinach
- 2 garlic
- 1 onion
- 3 tablespoons of soya sauce
- 1 tablespoon of sesame oil
- Pinch of Salt
- 1 tablespoon of cut ginger

For the sauce:
- 2 cups of soya sauce
- 3 tablespoons of wine oil

Methods:

1. From water and flour prepare the dough. Let it sit for close to 30 minutes.

2. Wash the spinach, cook it in water for a few minutes. Dry it and cut into small pieces.

3. Cut onion and garlic.

4. In one bowl, mix meat, spinach, onion, garlic, soya sauce, sesame oil, ginger, and salt. Mix everything together. (If needed - add water)

5. Knead the dough, make roller shape and cut it into smaller pieces. Make small round shapes from each one.

6. Put 1 tablespoon of mixture on each one. Fold them in half and you will get something like pillows.

7. Cook these "pillows" in boiling water for 15 minutes.

8. Prepare sauce – mix wine oil with soya sauce. When the dough is done, spread this sauce over them and enjoy!

Recipe 25: Chicken with Honey

Total Prep Time: **60 minutes**

Yield: 4

List of Ingredients:

- 20 oz. of chicken meat
- 10 oz. of spaghetti
- 3 carrots
- 1 celery
- 2 tablespoons of oil
- 3 tablespoons of soya sauce
- 1 tablespoon of salt
- 2 tablespoons of cut parsley
- 1 tablespoon of pepper
- 1 tablespoon of mustard
- 1 cup of water

Methods:

1. Cut chicken into small cubes, add salt and pepper.

2. Mix mustard and honey. Spread the mixture over the chicken. Let it sit for 2 hours.

3. Cut vegetables into small cubes.

4. Put the meat in a cooking pot with 1 cup of water and vegetables. Cook until it gets soft.

5. Prepare the spaghetti, spiced with soya sauce.

6. Mix everything together and cook again for a few minutes.

7. Sprinke cut parsley onto the dish and serve!

Recipe 26: Spicy Vegetables

Total Prep Time: **40 minutes**

Yield: 4

List of Ingredients:

- 2 big potatoes
- 2 tablespoons of oil
- ½ cup of water
- 1 tablespoon of cut ginger
- 4 garlic
- 2 tablespoons of white wine
- 4 tablespoons of soya sauce
- 1 green bell pepper
- 1 red bell pepper
- 1 chili pepper
- 1 tablespoon of sesame oil

Methods:

1. Cut vegetables into slices. Cook the potato in boiling water for 1 minute.

2. In a frying pan, heat the oil, ginger and add potato. Fry just for a few minutes and then add peppers and onion.

3. Fry everything for 5 minutes.

4. Add soya sauce, water and wine. Cook for 1 more minute and then add sesame oil.

Recipe 27: "Mame"

Total Prep Time: **45 minutes**

Yield: 4

List of Ingredients:

- 1 onion
- 3 carrots
- 4 green bell peppers
- 1 zucchini
- ½ cabbage head
- 1 pack of noodles
- 1 garlic
- 1 tablespoons of sesame
- Spices to taste (soya sauce, pepper, salt, oregano...)
- 20 oz. of pork meat

Methods:

1. Cut meat and vegetables into lines. Grate the cabbage.

2. Heat the oil in a frying pan. Add meat and vegetables and stir fry them together for 30 minutes.

3. Add spices to taste.

4. Cook the noodles. When they are done, strain them.

5. Add noodles into the frying pan and stir fry for 2 more minutes.

6. Bon apetit!

Recipe 28: Spicy Eggplants

Total Prep Time: **50 minutes**

Yield: 5

List of Ingredients:

- 2 eggplants
- 1 onion
- 2 garlic
- 1 tablespoon of oil
- 1 tablespoon of chili pepper
- 2 tablespoons of soya sauce
- 1 tablespoon of sesame oil

Methods:

1. Wash and peel eggplants. Cut them into small cubes.

2. Do the same with garlic and onion.

3. Heat the oil in a frying pan and add eggplants with salt. Fry just for a few minutes.

4. In the same oil, stir fry onion, garlic, and chili pepper.

5. After 5 minutes, put eggplants back into the frying pan with soya sauce and sesame oil.

6. Serve this meal with rice and enjoy!

Recipe 29: Three colors meal

Green and red pepper, and color of meat are what makes this three colors and this delicious meal!

Total Prep Time: **30 minutes**

Yield: 4

List of Ingredients:

- 14 oz. of chicken meat
- 1 tablespoon of salt
- 1 tablespoon of soya sauce
- 1 tablespoon of cut ginger
- 1 tablespoon of cut garlic
- 10 oz. of red bell pepper
- 7 oz. of green bell pepper
- 2 tablespoons of oil
- 1 tablespoon of sesame oil

Methods:

1. Cut meat into small pieces. Fry it in a hot oil. When it is done, remove it from the frying pan.

2. Peel the peppers and cut them into small pieces.

3. In the same oil, add cut garlic, ginger, peppers and fry everything together for close to 3 minutes.

4. Put the meat back and then add the soya sauce, salt, pepper, sesame oil. Mix everything and stir fry for few more minutes.

5. Serve it with rice and enjoy!

Recipe 30: Chicken with Celery

Total Prep Time: **45 minutes**

Yield: 2

List of Ingredients:

- 7 oz. of chicken meat
- 1 tablespoon of salt
- 1 tablespoon of pepper
- ½ cup of oil
- ½ cup of water
- 1 tablespoon of garlic
- 2 tablespoons of ginger
- ½ cup of white wine
- 1 egg white
- 4 celery
- 1 tablespoon of sesame oil
- 1 tablespoon of curry sauce

Methods:

1. Cut ginger and garlic into small pieces.

2. Cut celery leaf into lines and cook it in water for close to 2 minutes.

3. Mix ginger, garlic, white wine, water, salt and pepper.

4. Cut meat into lines (or cubes).

5. In one bowl, mix egg white with curry sauce and pour that mixture over the meat.

6. Fry meat in a frying pan. Add celery and ginger/garlic mixture – fry it together.

7. When the meat is ready, add sesame oil and enjoy!

Part 2

Introduction

I want to thank you and congratulate you for downloading the book, Vegan Mastery Cookbook: Simple Chinese Vegan Recipes to Cook at Home (International Vegan Cookbook Series).

Vegan Mastery Cookbook: Simple Chinese Vegan Recipes to Cook at Home is your one-stop source for creating the perfect Chinese appetizers, entrees and desserts for your friends and family.

Inside you will be treated to a wide selection of vegan Chinese recipes, making it easy to satisfy all preferences. There are recipes that will suit every palate on any occasion whether it is fall, spring, summer, or winter.

Vegan "Egg" Drop Soup

Ingredients

2 Cups Vegetable Broth

5 Oz Finely Sliced Packet of Silken Tofu

4 Shitake Mushrooms-sliced thin

1/2 Inch Piece of Ginger Finely Grated

1 Garlic Clove-finely grated

1 Tablespoon Rice Wine Vinegar

1 Teaspoon Sesame Oil

1 Stalk of Finely Diced Scallion

½ Tablespoon Soy Sauce (or Tamari Sauce)

Sriracha to Taste

Preparation

In a sauce pan, add all ingredients except tofu and scallions. Bring to a boil.

Next, add tofu slowly and stir. Reduce to a simmer.

Check for seasoning. If soup needs flavor add more Soy Sauce or Tamari Sauce.

Add scallions and serve!

Vegan Hot and Sour Soup

Ingredients

8-ounce Chinese Noodles (follow instructions on package)

2 Tablespoons Sunflower Oil or Canola Oil

2 Garlic Cloves-minced

½ Teaspoon Fresh Ginger-minced

½ Teaspoon Dried Chili Flakes

4 Cups Vegetable Broth

1 Tablespoon Tamari Sauce or Soy Sauce

¼ Teaspoon Ground White Pepper

3 Tablespoons Chinese Black Vinegar (find at local Asian markets)

½ Teaspoon Toasted Sesame Oil

3 Tablespoons Potato Starch

¼ Cup Bok Choy-chopped

¼ Cup Fresh Shiitake Mushrooms-hard stems removed

1 Small Carrot-julienned

3-ounce Firm Tofu-diced into 1/2-inch cubes

2 Medium Scallions-finely chopped

1 Tablespoon Cilantro-chopped

Preparation

Boil Chinese noodles according to package instructions. After noodles are cooked, remove nooldes from the pot and place them in a tray full of cold water. Set aside.

In a large pot, heat oil, and sauté garlic and ginger on medium heat until fragrant. Add dried chili flakes. Then, pour in broth.

Next, add white pepper, sesame oil, Chinese black vinegar, and soy sauce into the pot and stir for 3 minutes.

Next, add all vegetables & tofu and allow to cook for 8-10 minutes.

Meanwhile, in a separate bowl, dissolve starch in ½ cup cold water until smooth and then add to soup while it is boiling. Stir continually.

Prepare your cooked noodles in serving bowls. Add the soup to the serving bowls.

Garnish with cilantro and green onions and serve!

Chinese "Chicken" Salad

Ingredients

2 packages vegan "chicken" strips-***diced***

1 Head of Lettuce-cut into small pieces
4 Green Onions-diced thin
4 Celery Stalks-sliced thin
1/2 Cup Walnuts-chopped
2 Tablespoons Toasted Sesame Seeds
6 Ounces Chinese Noodles-heated briefly to crisp
6 Tablespoons Seasoned Rice Vinegar
4 Tablespoons White Sugar or Stevia
1 Teaspoon Salt
1/2 Cup Peanut Oil

Preparation

In a large salad bowl, combine "chicken" strips, lettuce, green onion, nuts, celery, seeds and noodles. Mix together. and set aside.

Dressing Preparation: Add vinegar into a small bowl. Dissolve sugar and salt in vinegar then add oil. Beat well.

Add dressing to salad and toss.

Serve and enjoy!

Steamed Dumplings

Ingredients

1/2 Cup Mushrooms-finely chopped
1/2 cup Grated Carrots
1/2 Cup Cabbage-shredded
2 Tablespoon Red Pepper-finely chopped
2 Tablespoon Onion-finely chopped
2 Teaspoons Fresh Ginger-minced
1 Tablespoon Soy Sauce or Tamari Sauce
1 Tablespoon Sesame Oil
Salt and pepper-to taste
Approximately 40 small dumpling wrapper

Preparation

In a large bowl, combine carrots, mushrooms, cabbage, red pepper, onion, ginger, soy sauce (or tamari sauce), and sesame oil. Stir and season with salt and pepper.

Form the dumplings by individually placing the wrappers on a dry working surface. Place 1 teaspoon of vegetable mixture in the center of the wrapper. Next, wet the edges of the wrapper with water and proceed to fold one side over and pinch edges until sealed. Repeat until all of the filling is gone.

Next, bring approximately half inch of water to a simmer over medium heat. In a steamer, place as many dumplings as possible without them touching each other. Cover and steam for 10 to 12 minutes. Repeat until all dumplings are cooked.

Serve dumplings hot with a side of hoisin sauce or sauce of your choice.

Vegan Fried Rice

Ingredients

2 cups rice

3 Tablespoons Vegetable Oil

¾ Cup Green Beans-finely chopped

2 Carrots-finely chopped

1 Onion-sliced

¾ Cups Finely Chopped Cabbage

1 Teaspoon Garlic-finely chopped

2 Tablespoons Tamari Sauce or Soy Sauce

1 Tablespoon Vinegar

Salt and Pepper-to taste

Preparation

Cook rice according to directions on package. Next, heat oil in large pan and stir fry all of the chopped vegetables. Cook for 3 – 5 minutes. Add salt and pepper to taste.

Add cooked rice to vegetables and mix. Next, add soy sauce and vinegar. Cook the fried rice for approximately 3 minutes.

Serve fried rice and enjoy!

Ginger Teriyaki Noodles

Ingredients

2 Tablespoons Teriyaki Sauce

2 Tablespoons Soy Sauce

2 Tablespoons Wine Vinegar

2 Tablespoons Ground Ginger

2 Celery Stalks-diced

1 Carrot-diced

½ Onion-diced

2/3 Cup Snow Peas

4 Scallions-sliced

3 Tablespoons Olive Oil

1 Tablespoon Sesame Oil

1 Pound Chinese-Style Noodles or Lo Mein Noodles

Preparation

Mix the soy sauce, teriyaki sauce, vinegar and ginger together and set aside.

Then, cook the Chinese noodles until soft, about 6 to 8 minutes. Drain well.

In a large wok, sautee the vegetables in 2 tablespoons of the olive oil for 4 to 5 minutes until tender.

Add remaining oil and the teriyaki and soy sauce mixture to the skillet. Next, add the Chinese noodles. Allow to cook for another 6 minutes, stirring continuously.

Serve and enjoy!

Vegan Chinese Noodles

Ingredients

1 Pound Asian Noodles or Spaghetti

5 Green Onions-sliced

4 Garlic Cloves-minced

½ Teaspoon Olive Oil

½ Cup Vegetable Broth

1/ Teaspoon Cornstarch

1/3 Cup Soy Sauce or Tamari Sauce

2 Tablespoons Ketchup

1 Tablespoon Vinegar

1 Tablespoon Chili Sauce (Sriracha or Hot Sauce)

1 Teaspoon Sugar or Stevia

1/3 Cup Peanuts

1 Cucumber-sliced thin

Preparation

First, cook the spaghetti or Asian noodles according to the instructions on the package.

Next, in a large wok, sautee the garlic and green onions for two minutes. Next, add the remaining ingredients (except the peanuts and cucumber) and whisk together.

Then, add the cucumber, peanuts, and noodles, stirring well. Cook until heated all the way through.

Plate and serve!

Chinese Pear and Avocado Bowl

Ingredients

½ Avocado-pitted, peeled, and diced

1 15-oz. Can of Chickpeas-drained

1 Asian pear (med-sized)-cored and sliced thin

2 celery Stalks-chopped

1 Cup Cucumber-diced

1 Jalapeño Chili (small)-stemmed, seeded, and minced

¼ Cup Cilantro-chopped

1 Tablespoon Canola Oil

2 Tablespoons Fresh Lime Juice

Preparation

Combine all ingredients into a bowl. Season with salt and pepper.

Serve and enjoy!

Spicy Sesame Peanut Noodles

Ingredients

¼ Cup Soy Sauce or Tamari Sauce

2/3 Cup Peanut Butter

3 Garlic Cloves-minced

2 Green Onions-diced

2 Tablespoons Sesame Oil

½ Teaspoon Ginger Powder

½ Teaspoon Cayenne Pepper Powder

1 Lime-juiced

½ Pound Asian Noodles or Spaghetti

2 Tablespoons Sesame Seeds

Preparation

First, cook noodles according to the package directions. Heat pan to low heat and add all ingredients (except noodles and sesame seeds). Stir together carefully.

Next, pour the sauce that is in the pan over the noodles gently tossing to combine. Add the sesame seeds on top.

Serve hot or cold and enjoy!

Vegetable Lo Mein

Ingredients

8 Ounces of Udon or Soba Noodles

5 Green Onions

3 Garlic Cloves-minced

1 ½ Tablespoons Fresh Ginger-grated

½ Teaspoon Red Pepper Flakes

1 Cup Mushrooms-sliced

1 Handful Snow Peas

1 Can Bamboo Shoots-drained

2 Yellow Squash-thinly sliced

3 Carrots-thinly sliced

½ Cup Vegetable Broth

1 ½ Teaspoon Salt

Lo Mein Sauce Ingredients

-

2 Teaspoons Rice Vinegar

4 Tablespoons Soy Sauce or Tamari Sauce

¼ Teaspoon Ground Ginger

¼ Teaspoon Garlic Powder

½ Teaspoon Agave Nectar

½ Teaspoon Hot Sauce (i.e. Sriracha)

½ Teaspoon Vegetable Oil

Preparation

First, prepare the noodles according to the package instructions.

Next, prepare the sauce by cooking sauce ingredients over low heat for a few minutes until all ingredients are blended well. In a hot pan/wok, add the broth and stir fry the veggies until tender. Next, add the cooked noodles to the wok/pan. Stir all ingredients together. Then, pour the Lo Mein sauce over the top and fry a few minutes longer stirring continuously.

Plate the dish, sprinkle with minced dark green section of onions, and serve!

Eggplant and Potato Chinese Dish

Ingredients

-
1 Eggplant-sliced into cubes
1 Green Pepper-diced
1 Potato-peeled and cut into squares
2 Garlic Cloves-chopped
1 Tablespoon of Soy Sauce or Tamari Sauce
Salt, sugar/Stevia, Oil

Preparation

First choose an eggplant that is heavy and firm with an even dark color.

Pat the eggplant dry with a paper towel before cooking it. Slice and salt the eggplant.

There are dozens of ways to cook the eggplant. Options include deep-frying, grilling, baking, steaming, sauté, pickling, etc. Keep in mind that the eggplant soaks up oil like a sponge, especially good olive oil.

Saute the potatoes and eggplant separately in a pan with oil until each golden brown. Remove each and drain.

Next, stir-fry the green peppers with a tablespoon of oil in a separate pan for a few minutes.

Add the cooked eggplant and potatoes to the green peppers, along with the soy sauce or tamari sauce, chopped garlic, salt and a pinch of sugar/stevia.

Continue to stir fry for a few minutes then remove from heat.

Serve hot and enjoy!

Vegan Orange Chicken

Ingredients

1 package of Gardein Mandarin Orange Chick'n

1 "boil in a bag" rice (brown or wild)

2 Tablespoons Hoisin Sauce

Assorted Vegetables-fresh or frozen stir-fry style

¼ Cup Sweet Chili Sauce

2 Tablespoons Olive Oil

Preparation

First, boil rice then set aside. Then, place Gardein sauce packet in warm water to thaw and set aside.

Next, heat olive oil in a pan on medium high and add "chick'n" to pan and cook until slightly crisp.

Add assorted vegetables to the same pan- cook until slightly crisp and tender.

Next, add Gardein sauce to the chicken & vegetables and mix well. Then, add the hoisin sauce & sweet chili sauce to the mixture.

Place mixture over rice and serve!

Kung Pao "Chicken" & Vegetables

Ingredients

¾ Cup Diced Carrots

8 Ounces Mushrooms-sliced

¾ Cup Celery-sliced

¾ Cup Onion-diced

1 package of vegan "chicken"

8 Ounces Water Chestnuts-diced

½ Cup Dry Roasted Peanuts (optional)

3 Garlic Cloves-minced

3 Stalks Bok Choy-diced

3 Teaspoons Rice Wine/Sake

3 Teaspoons Soy Sauce or Tamari

2 Teaspoons Rice Vinegar

2 Teaspoons Cornstarch in ¼ Cup Water

Sriracha (hot sauce) to taste

Preparation

Place the sliced mushrooms in a pan and stir until mushrooms are released of their liquid. Add celery, carrots, and onions and cook until colors of vegetables brighten. Next, add peanuts (optional), water chestnuts, Bok Choy, and garlic and cook until heated all the way through.

In a separate bowl, mix together the soy sauce (or tamari sauce), rice vinegar, and rice wine. Then, pour over the vegetables, mix together, and cook until mix bubbles slightly. Then, add the cornstarch that has been dissolved in water to thicken the sauce.

Add the Sriracha to taste and serve over rice!

"Chicken" and Broccoli

Ingredients

2 Tablespoons Sesame Oil

6 Garlic Cloves-minced

¼ Cup Soy Sauce or Tamari Sauce

1-1/2 Cups Vegetable Broth

¼ Cup Mirin (sweet rice wine)

1 Tablespoon Agave

½ Teaspoon Hoisin Sauce

2 Teaspoons Cornstarch

2 Packages Vegan Chicken-diced

Brown or White Rice "Boil in a Bag"

Preparation

Prepare the rice according to package instructions and set aside.

Then, blanch the broccoli (cook in boiling water for a few minutes). Drain broccoli and run under cold water so it stays bright green.

Heat sesame oil in a large pan. Next, add the garlic and cook until lightly browned.

Add soy sauce (or tamari sauce), vegetable broth, mirin, hoisin sauce, and agave, then stir to combine. Cook for approximately seven minutes.

Then, mix a small amount of the sauce with the corn starch to make a slurry. Then add it to the sauce. Next, add the vegan chicken and cook, stirring continuously, until cooked all the way through.

Next, add in the broccoli and stir to combine.

Serve with rice and enjoy!

"Beef" and Broccoli Stir Fry

Ingredients

4 Ounces Tempeh-cut into 1/2-inch pieces

1/4 Cup Soy Sauce or Tamari Sauce

1 Tablespoon Rice Vinegar

3 Garlic Cloves-minced

2 Teaspoons Fresh Ginger-peeled and minced

1 Pinch Dried Crushed Red Pepper

12 Ounces Broccoli-stems peeled and cut into 1/2-inch pieces & florets cut into 1-inch pieces

2 Tablespoons Water

1 Teaspoon Agave

1 Teaspoon Cornstarch

1 Tablespoon Vegetable Oil

1/2 Cup Red Bell Pepper-chopped

2 Tablespoons Green Onion-thinly sliced

Preparation

Stir ginger, tempeh, soy sauce, vinegar, garlic, and crushed red pepper and chopped red bell pepper in a bowl and mix ingredients. Allow to marinate for one hour at room temperature.

Next, steam the broccoli for approximately 3 minutes and set aside. Then, strain the marinade from tempeh into small bowl and set the tempeh aside.

Whisk the 2 tablespoons water, agave and cornstarch into marinade.

Next, heat oil in large pan over high heat. Add the marinated bell pepper and tempeh and cook for 4 minutes. Add broccoli and marinade mixture and sauté until broccoli is heated through for approximately 3 minutes. Transfer to bowl.

Plate, top with green onion, and serve!

Chicken and Mushroom Stir Fry

Ingredients

2 Packages of Vegan "Chicken"

½ Pound Mushrooms (med-sized)

2 Garlic Cloves

1 ½ Tablespoons Vegetable Oil for cooking

1 Teaspoon Sesame Oil

Salt and Pepper-to taste

Marinade Ingredients

3 Tablespoons Soy Sauce or Tamari Sauce

1 Tablespoon Cornstarch

1 Teaspoon Sugar

Preparation

First, if vegan chicken is not already sliced, slice into thin pieces. Next, in a bowl, combine "chicken" pieces with the marinade ingredients. Mix together and set aside.

Wash the mushrooms and slice into ¼ inch thin pieces. Then, crush, peel, and finely chop the garlic. Heat 1 tablespoon oil in a pan over medium-high heat. When oil is hot, add the marinated vegan chicken into pan. Cook and stir for approximately 3 minutes until the "chicken" is just about cooked through. Transfer "chicken" onto a plate or bowl and set aside. Add ½ tablespoon oil into the pan. Brown the garlic for a few seconds then add the sliced mushrooms, salt and pepper to pan. Cook and stir the mushrooms for about 1 to 2 minutes until the mushrooms are soft. Add the cooked chicken back into the pan and mix. Add sesame oil and cook for a few seconds longer.

Serve dish hot and enjoy!

Vegan Sweet and Sour "Chicken"

Ingredients for the Marinade

2 Packages Vegan "Chicken" Strips-cut into bite-sized pieces
1 Tablespoon Arrowroot Powder
2 Tablespoons Tamari Sauce or Soy Sauce

Ingredients for the Dish

2 Tablespoons Oil

2 Garlic Cloves-minced

2 Teaspoons Fresh Ginger-grated

2 Bell Peppers-chopped

8 Ounces Pineapple Chunks

Ingredients for the Sweet and Sour Sauce

½ Onion (medium-sized)-chopped

2 Garlic Cloves-minced

2 Teaspoons Fresh Ginger-grated

Extra Juice from the Pineapple (can or package)

⅓ Cup Ketchup

¼ Cup Brown Rice Vinegar

¼ Cup Stevia or Sugar

2 Tablespoons Tamari Sauce or Soy Sauce

2 Teaspoon Arrowroot Powder

¼ Cup Water

Preparation

To prepare the marinade: In a bowl, combine the vegan chicken strips, arrowroot powder and tamari or soy sauce and mix. Allow to marinate for at least 30 minutes.

To make the Sweet and Sour Sauce: In a saucepan over medium heat, add the onions and cook 2 minutes until softened. Then, add the garlic and ginger stirring for approximately 30 seconds. Next, add the pineapple juice, ketchup, tamari sauce or soy sauce, brown rice vinegar, and the sugar/Stevia. Bring to a simmer and cook, stirring occasionally, for approximately 3-4 minutes. In a separate bowl, mix the arrowroot and water until smooth. Then, add to the sauce and bring to a boil. Allow to cook for 1 minute then turn off heat and set aside.

To make the Sweet and Sour "Chicken": Heat oil in a pan over med-heat. Add the vegan chicken strips to the pan and cook (turn once) until crisp and slightly browned for approximately 4-5 minutes. Add additional oil to the pan if needed and cook the garlic and ginger for 2 minutes until softened stirring continuously and tossing to coat the vegan chicken strips. Then, add the bell peppers and pineapple chunks. Cook until the pineapple is slightly crisp and pepper are tender for approximately 3-4 minutes.

Next, stir in the sweet and sour sauce mixture into the pan and coat all vegan chicken strips and veggies. Bring to a boil and allow to cook until sauce is thick for approximately 2 minutes.

Serve with rice and enjoy!

8 TREASURE RICE PUDDING

The traditional Chinese New Year rice pudding dish Americanized and Veganized!

Ingredients

2 cups forbidden rice

3/4 cups dried fruit; prunes, apricots, cherries, etc.

1/2 cup adzuki beans (For optimal heath, adzuki beans should be spouted and slow cooked, however, canned beans will work for this recipe.)

1/2 cup water

1/4 vanilla bean

1/4 tsp cinnamon

Topping Ingredient

1 Can Coconut Cream or Coconut Vanilla Ice Cream

Preparation

Rinse forbidden rice for approximately 2 minutes.

Cook forbidden rice according to package instructions.

Next, blend up beans, dried fruit, and water to make a fruit and bean paste.

Then, add the fruit and bean paste to the rice and stir ingredients.

Form rice by packing it down with a spoon in a large bowl. Optional: Create layers with nuts, fresh fruit, caramel, coconut shreds etc.

Top with the coconut cream or coconut vanilla ice cream and serve!

Vegan Almond Cookies

Ingredients

1 Cup Shortening

¼ Teaspoon Salt

3 Cups Flour

1 Teaspoon Baking Soda

¼ Cup Soymilk

1 Cup Sugar or Stevia

2 Teaspoons Almond Extract

Blanched Almonds

Preparation

Cut shortening into the dry ingredients(salt, flour, baking soda, sugar or Stevia). Then, add soy milk and almond extract and mix well. Knead until soft.

Next, form into balls the size of a walnut. Flatten slightly with hand and place on cookie sheet. Press a blanched almond on each cookie.

Bake at 350 for 10 to 15 minutes (watching constantly to not overcook).

Serve to guests and enjoy!

Chinese lunch Recipes

Chinese Fried Rice

What ingredients you will need:

3/4 cup finely chopped onion
2 1/2 tablespoons oil
2 tablespoons soy sauce
2 cups beans sprouts
4 green onions chopped
4 cups cold cooked rice
1/2 cup frozen peas, thawed
1/2 cup finely chopped carrot
8 ounces chopped cooked meat
3 drops sesame oil
3 drops soy sauce
1 beaten egg

Directions:

1) In a wok, heat 1tbsp oil and add onions (chopped) to it. Until the onions don't turn light brown, keeping stirring them (this will take about 8-11 minutes).

2) Once they are done, remove them from the wok.

3) Let the wok cool a bit. Take 3 drops of sesame oil and 3 drops of soya and mix an egg with it and put aside.

4)   In the wok, take ½ tbsp of oil and coat the facade by swirling it. Mix in the egg combination and swirl until the eggs set properly around the surfaces of the wok.

5)   Flip the side when the eggs start to puff and cook the other side properly. After it's done, remove it from the wok and chop in pieces.

6) Take 1tbsp oil and heat in wok. Add the meat, carrots, peas, onion and sauté them for around 2 minutes.

7) Add in rice, bean sprouts and green onions and toss them properly so that they are mixed well. Stir for around 3 minutes.

8)   In the rice mixture, add 2tbsp of light soy sauce and chopped egg and fold them in. Stir fry for another 1 minute and dish up! If you want, you can place some soy sauce separately with it!

9)   Serve and enjoy. This recipe will give you 4 serving in total.

Nutritional facts per serving:

Serving size: 400g

Calories: 500kcal

Carbohydrates: 62g

Protein: 26g

Fat: 15g

Fiber: 4g

Chinese Roasted Chicken

What ingredients you will need:

1 1/2 kg chicken pieces

1/3 cup dark soy sauce

1 tablespoon five-spice powder

1 tablespoon honey

1 tablespoon grated gingerroot

1 tablespoon crushed garlic

1 tablespoon sesame oil

Directions:

1) Marinate the chicken for 2 hours at minimum with all the mentioned ingredients. Toss them up and down frequently.

2) Take a roasting dish and arrange the chicken pieces in a single layer and bake for 30 minutes in oven (160 C/ 325 F). Twist the pieces and roast them for 25 minutes more.

3) You can serve it anyway you want to; hot or cold!

4) Serve and enjoy. This recipe will give you 6 serving in total.

Nutritional facts per serving:

Serving size: 270g

Calories: 580kcal

Carbohydrates: 4g

Protein: 48g

Fat: 11g

Fiber: 1g

Chinese Chicken with Black Pepper Sauce

What ingredients you will need:

Stir-Fry

1 cup frozen peas and carrot

cooking oil

hot steamed rice

1 lb boneless skinless chicken thighs

1 large diced onion

6 tablespoons cornstarch

For the Sauce

1 teaspoon dark soy sauce

1 teaspoon black pepper

1/2 teaspoon white pepper

1/4 cup oyster sauce

1 teaspoon sake

Directions:

1) Mix the sauce components in a bowl and put it aside.

2) Cut down the chicken in ¼ inch shaped dice.

3) In a bowl, take cornstarch and powder the chicken piece in it. Shake off the extra cornstarch.

4) Heat oil and fry them until they are golden brown and crispy; this will take about 2-3 minutes (drain the excessive oil). Dispose of the used oil from the wok.

5) In a wok, heat oil and add in onions to it, stir frying them for a minute. Put in carrots and peas and cook for 30 seconds further.

6) Now, add in the sauce combination and the fried chicken pieces. Mix well to coat all the elements evenly.

7) Serve right away (preferred with steam rice).

8) Serve and enjoy. This recipe will give you 3 serving in total.

Nutritional facts per serving:

Serving size: 220g

Calories: 300kcal

Carbohydrates: 28g

Protein: 35g

Fat: 7g

Fiber: 3g

Chinese Beef With Broccoli

What ingredients you will need:

1/2 kg beef sirloin tip, sliced thinly into strips
2 tablespoons cornstarch
1/4 cup kikoman soy sauce
1/4 cup rice wine
1 -2 tablespoon cooking oil

1/4 cup water

1 pinch baking soda

2 teaspoons oyster sauce

1 head broccoli

2 green onions

1 tablespoon sugar

Directions:

1) With the back of a knife, pound the meat slices and put them sideways.

2) Take cornstarch and rice wine and combine them.

3) Marinate the meat slices with the cornstarch and rice wine combination for 30 minutes.

4) Merge together Kikkoman Soy sauce and sugar and put them aside.

5) In the meantime, cut down the broccoli into tiny florets and cut the stems slantwise. Dispose the bog stalk.

6) Turn on the flame at medium heat and heat oil in a wok. Now add in the marinated beef and stir it.

7) Mix it well until the beef slices start to change color. Don't change its color to a large extend (it should be half done).

8) Mix in the Kikkoman and sugar mixture. Further add in oyster sauce, broccoli and mix for 5 minutes or until you sense that it's done completely.

9) While it's cooking, add only a pinch of baking soda to it.

10) Mix in ¼ cup of water and cook for at least a minute more.

11) Serve and enjoy. This recipe will give you 4 serving in total.

Nutritional facts per serving:

Serving size: 230g

Calories: 150kcal

Carbohydrates: 20g

Protein: 7g

Fat: 4g
Fiber: 5g

Chinese Grilled Chicken

What ingredients you will need:

1/4 cup lemon juice

3 tablespoons olive oil

2 boneless skinless chicken breasts

1/4 teaspoon ground ginger

5 tablespoons soy sauce

1 tablespoon honey

2 tablespoons hoisin sauce

1 chopped garlic clove

Directions:

1) Take a plastic bag and merge all the ingredients in it (leaving the chicken behind).

2) To make the chicken infuse all the goods, bash it properly and then adjoin to the liquid. Put into the refrigerator for some hours.

3) Take the chicken out of the combination and grill it evenly for best taste.

4) Serve and enjoy. This recipe will give you 2 serving in total.

Nutritional facts per serving:

Serving size: 240g

Calories: 400kcal

Carbohydrates: 20g

Protein: 30g

Fat: 24g

Fiber: 1g

Chinese Spicy Beef Lettuce Wraps

What ingredients you will need:

2 heads lettuce

1 tablespoon cold water

1 teaspoon cornstarch

1 jalapeno chili minced

1 (8 ounce) can water chestnuts

1 bunch green onions

1/2 teaspoon Chinese five spice powder

1 teaspoon thai chili paste

1 tablespoon dark sesame oil

3 tablespoons soy sauce

2 minced garlic cloves

1 lb lean ground beaf

Directions:

1) Take large and heavy skillet with the help of a non sticking cooking spray. Over medium flame, brown ground beef in the skillet and drain it if you feel the need to.

2) Add in the further ingredients; sherry, garlic, soy sauce, chili paste, sesame oil, five-spice powder, water chestnuts, white part of green onions and minced chile.

3) Turn the flame to low heat and let the mixture simmer for 10 minutes.

4) Make a cornstarch mixture and add it to the beef combination and keep stirring it unless it starts to condense.

5) Mix in the green parts of the green onions and cook it properly.

6) Wash the lettuce leaves and pat and dry them appropriately.

7) Arrange the lettuce cups beautifully along the platter with the beef combination. A must serving for this is the Sweet Soy Dipping Sauce!

5) Serve and enjoy. This recipe will give you 5 serving in total.

Nutritional facts per serving:

Serving size: 240g

Calories: 267kcal

Carbohydrates: 16g

Protein: 21g

Fat: 12g

Fiber: 3g

Ground Beef Chinese Style

What ingredients you will need:

1 lb lean ground beef

1 cup macaroni

2 ounces soya sauce

1 1/2 cups beef broth

1/2 cup chopped bell pepper

1 cup sliced mushrooms

1 cup chopped celery

2 crushed garlic cloves

1 cup chopped onion

Directions:

1) In a cast iron skillet add meat and cook it until it becomes brown. Now add all vegetables in it. Cook until vegetables become soft.

2) Reduce heat and simmer for five minutes.

3) Now add all remaining ingredients in it and cook until macaroni is cooked completely.

4) Serve and enjoy. This recipe will give you 4 serving in total.

Nutritional facts per serving:
Serving size: 340g
Calories: 300kcal
Carbohydrates: 26g
Protein: 30g
Fat: 12g
Fiber: 3g

Chinese Sesame Limas

What ingredients you will need:

2 tablespoons peanut oil

1 teaspoon sesame oil

1 (10 ounce) package frozen large lima beans

1 teaspoon salt

1 tablespoon sugar

1/2 cup chicken broth

Directions:

1) Discard the limas from its packet and allow it to defrost. Separate with the help of your fingers.

2) Place a skillet over high flame and let it heat up. Once it's hot add in the peanut oil and stir for 20-30 seconds.

3) Throw in the beans and sauté them until they change their color to icy green. For seasoning, spray in salt and sugar and briskly stir them properly for around half a minute. Now, add in stock/water and let it simmer over medium flame.

4) Cover the skillet (but not completely; leave a space open) and let it cook for 5 minutes.

5) Uncover it so that the remaining liquid is allowed to evaporate and keep stirring it constantly.

6) Insert the sesame oil and cook it for some seconds so that it is evenly distributed. Serve hot!

7) Serve and enjoy. This recipe will give you 4 serving in total.

Nutritional facts per serving:

Serving size: 110g

Calories: 120kcal

Carbohydrates: 12g

Protein: 4g

Fat: 12g

Fiber: 3g

Chinese Spaghetti

What ingredients you will need:

1 (8 ounce) package spaghetti

1/4 teaspoon crushed red pepper flakes

1/4 cup soy sauce

1 medium shredded carrot

3 chopped green onions

1/2 lb sliced mushrooms

1/4 cup extra virgin olive oil

Directions:

1) Cook the spaghetti, drain it and then put it back in the saucepan to keep it warm. \

2) Place a skillet over medium flame and add in mushrooms, onions and carrots in hot oil and let them cook. Let it cook until the ingredients get crispy and tender.

3) Add the vegetable combination into the saucepan containing the spaghetti. Put in crushed red pepper and soy sauce.

4) Mix and toss evenly with care, to combine all the elements. Serve it as you wish; warm or chill!

5) Serve and enjoy. This recipe will give you 6 serving in total.

Nutritional facts per serving:

Serving size: 110g

Calories: 220kcal

Carbohydrates: 31g

Protein: 8g

Fat: 10g

Fiber: 3g

Chinese Chicken Manchurian

What ingredients you will need:

2 tablespoons corn flour dissolved in 1/4 cup water
1/4 teaspoon ajinomoto
1 lb chicken meat cut into cubes
1 beaten egg
1 1/2 tablespoons corn flour
1/4 teaspoon salt
1/4 teaspoon sugar
1/4 teaspoon ground black pepper
1 tablespoon soy sauce
1 cup chicken stock
2 tablespoons chopped cilantro
2 tablespoons crushed green chili peppers
2 tablespoons crushed ginger
2 tablespoons crushed garlic

Directions:

1) For the batter; mix in corn flour, flour, salt and pepper with an egg (beaten).

2) Dip the chicken pieces in the marinade and fry them until they obtain a golden brown color. Keep sideways.

3) Heat oil in a pan for the Manchurian sauce and add in garlic and ginger. Fry them until they change color slightly.

4) Put in cilantro leaves and green chilies and fry them further for about a minute. Turn down the flame a bit.

5) Add in chicken stock, soya sauce, salt, sugar, ajinomoto and pepper. Simmer for at least 5 minutes.

6) Mix in corn flour with water and add to the mixture and let it boil. Stir in the fried chicken and cook for a minute or two and serve hot!

7) Serve and enjoy. This recipe will give you 4 serving in total.

Nutritional facts per serving:

Serving size: 230g

Calories: 290kcal

Carbohydrates: 14g

Protein: 30g

Fat: 12g

Fiber: 1g

Chinese Dinner Recipes

Beefy Chinese Dumplings

What ingredients you will need:

1 (14 ounce) package wonton wrappers
1 egg
1 tablespoon vegetable oil
1 onion, minced
1 carrot, shredded
1 tablespoon soy sauce
2 cups shredded Chinese cabbage
1 teaspoon salt
1 teaspoon sugar
1 1/2 pounds ground beef

Directions:

1) Combine together cabbage, carrot, beef and onion in a large sized bowl. Add in salt, sugar, egg, soy sauce and vegetable oil and stir.

2) Take a large teaspoon of this marinade and fill the center of the dumpling skin with it. With the help of water (only a few drops) dampen the edges of the wonton.

3) Fold the dumpling and close it by pinching the edges. Now create a ripple pattern on the pinched sides by pushing jointly all sections of it.

4)   Do the same with the remaining dumplings.

5)   Boil the dumplings in water for about 5 minutes or unless they start to rise above the surface.

6) Serve and enjoy. This recipe will give you 10 serving in total.

Nutritional facts per serving:

Serving size: 240g

Calories: 350kcal

Carbohydrates: 24g

Protein: 16g

Fat: 20g

Fiber: 1g

Chinese Scallion Pancakes

What ingredients you will need:

1 bunch green onions (scallions), minced
vegetable oil, or as needed, divided
1/2 cup cold water, or as needed
3/4 cup boiling water
1 tablespoon salt, divided
2 cups all-purpose flour

Directions:

1) In a large bowl, mix in a tablespoon of salt and flour and add in boiling water. Briskly stir it quickly until the water starts to absorb.

2) Add in cold water (only a teaspoon at a time) to the flour mixture until you obtain beautiful dough.

3) Press dough for minimum 10 minutes. Let the dough rest for 40 minutes by covering it with a damp cloth.

4) Dust flour on a surface and turn out your dough on it. Cut it into 4 equivalent pieces.

5) Take a piece of dough and roll it into a large thin round and brush it lightly with vegetable oil.

6) Spray salt and green onions on it and fold one end of the dough over the other (forming a long scroll shape).

7) Take a scroll end and roll it into a disk. Repeat the process with every disk and let them rest for around 10 minutes.

8) In a skillet, heat vegetable oil over medium heat. Take a disk and roll it over a floured surface in a round shape.

9) Cook for 2-3 minutes in hot oil and set aside. Do the same with the remaining disks.

10) Serve and enjoy. This recipe will give you 10 serving in total.

Nutritional facts per serving:

Serving size: 250g

Calories: 360kcal

Carbohydrates: 44g

Protein: 10g

Fat: 14g

Fiber: 3g

Crab Rangoon

What ingredients you will need:

1 (14 ounce) package small won ton wrappers
2 (8 ounce) packages cream cheese, softened
1 teaspoon minced fresh ginger root
1/2 teaspoon chopped fresh cilantro
1 quart oil for frying
1 pound crabmeat, shredded
3 tablespoons dark soy sauce
1/2 teaspoon dried parsley

Directions:

1) In a skillet, bring oil to 350 degrees F. After that, combine cream cheese, soy sauce, ginger, garlic, parsley, cilantro and crabmeat in a small sized bowl.

2) Drop 1 teaspoon of the cream cheese mixture in the middle of wonton's wrapper. Fold and shape the wonton wrapper into a half moon or triangle, depending on the wrapper you have purchased.

3) Dampen the edges with the help of some drops of water and close it. Take a lightly moisten paper towel and let the wonton wrappers rest on it for a while.

4) Put in 3-4 wonton's to the heated oil and let them cook properly (until golden brown). Put sideways to drain the excessive oil and serve hot!

5) Serve and enjoy. This recipe will give you 10 serving in total.

Nutritional facts per serving:
Serving size: 270g
Calories: 390kcal
Carbohydrates: 24g
Protein: 17g
Fat: 24g
Fiber: 1g

Pumpkin Bread Recipe

What ingredients you will need:

1/8 teaspoon Chinese five-spice powder
1/2 teaspoon ground cinnamon
1 (15 ounce) can pumpkin puree
2 eggs
1 cup white sugar
1/2 cup unsalted butter, softened
3/4 cup chopped toasted walnuts
cooking spray
1 teaspoon baking soda
1 teaspoon baking powder
1 teaspoon salt
2 cups all-purpose flour
1/8 teaspoon ground allspice

Directions:

1) Heat up your over beforehand to 325 degrees F.

2) Take a 9x5 inch loaf pan and spray it lightly with cooking spray. In another bowl, mix together butter and sugar.

3) Whisk or stir properly so that it becomes light and fluffy. Add in eggs one by one and keep whisking until they combine evenly.

4) Whip in pumpkin puree, cinnamon, Chinese five spices and all spice powder and whisk the ingredients well.

5) Add in salt, baking powder and baking soda to the pumpkin combination and stir constantly to combine consistently.

6) Mix in walnuts (chopped). Pour the entire assault into the loaf pan.

7) Bake in oven for about an hour or until the center comes out clean by checking with a toothpick.

8) Serve and enjoy. This recipe will give you 8 serving in total.

Nutritional facts per serving:

Serving size: 200g

Calories: 300kcal

Carbohydrates: 30g

Protein: 5g

Fat: 12g

Fiber: 3g

Lighter Chicken Egg Foo Young

What ingredients you will need:

1 green onion, chopped, or to taste
1/2 cup finely chopped water chestnuts
1 dash soy sauce
4 egg whites
1/2 cup bean sprouts
2 chicken tenders, chopped

Directions:

1) Place a skillet (sprayed with cooking spray) over medium flame. Cook chicken for 5 minutes and stir evenly so that it no longer remains pink and catches a light brownish color.

2) With the help of a spatula, extend chicken pieces on the surface of the skillet and spray with cooking spray again if you feel the need to do so.

3) Take a separate bowl and beat egg whites with soy sauce. Add in bean sprouts, water, chestnuts and green onions.

4) Pour out this egg combination over the chicken pieces and let it cook. It will cook for at least 3 minutes or until the chicken in light brown.

5) Cook the other side evenly also and serve!

6) Serve and enjoy. This recipe will give you 2 serving in total.

Nutritional facts per serving:

Serving size: 100g

Calories: 140kcal

Carbohydrates: 7g

Protein: 20g

Fat: 2g

Fiber: 2g

Quick Chinese-Style Vermicelli

What ingredients you will need:

1 tablespoon soy sauce
1 clove garlic, minced
1 green onion, chopped
2 tablespoons vegetable oil
salt and pepper to taste
1 (8 ounce) package dried rice noodles
1/2 tablespoon chili sauce

Directions:

1) In a pot boil water and then cook rice and noodles in it for 3 minutes. Do not overcook it and after cooking it drain it.

2) Heat up oil in a skillet. Now add all ingredients in this skillet and stir fry them.

3) Serve and enjoy. This original recipe will give you 4 servings in total.

Nutritional facts per serving:
Serving size: 150g

Calories: 260kcal

Carbohydrates: 40g

Protein: 3g

Fat: 7g

Fiber: 2g

Stir-Fried Cabbage

What ingredients you will need:

1 pound shredded cabbage
1 tablespoon soy sauce
2 cloves garlic, minced
1 tablespoon vegetable oil
1 tablespoon vinegar

Directions:

1) Heat up oil in a skillet and then cook garlic in it and make it brown.

2) Now pour cabbage in it and cook it for 2 minutes after covering skillet. Now add remaining ingredients and cook until cabbage is tender. Usually it takes almost 2 minutes.

3) In final process of cooking try to cook cabbage on high heat.

4) Serve and enjoy. This original recipe will give you 4 servings in total.

Nutritional facts per serving:
Serving size: 50g

Calories: 65kcal
Carbohydrates: 7g
Protein: 3g
Fat: 3g
Fiber: 3g

Chinese Broccoli

What ingredients you will need:

1 tablespoon rice vinegar
2 cloves garlic, minced
1 teaspoon minced fresh ginger root
2 tablespoons soy sauce
1 tablespoon cornstarch
3 tablespoons hoisin sauce
2 tablespoons white sugar
1 bunch Gai Lan (Chinese broccoli), trimmed
1 tablespoon sesame oil

Directions:

1) In a pot boil salted water and then add broccoli. Cook broccoli unless it is tender.

2) Now drain broccoli set it aside.

3) Take a mixing bowl and mix all remaining ingredients in it and make sauce.

4) Pour this sauce on broccoli and mix it with broccoli.

5) Serve and enjoy. This original recipe will give you 4 servings in total.

Nutritional facts per serving:

Serving size: 60g

Calories: 125kcal

Carbohydrates: 20g

Protein: 3g

Fat: 4g

Fiber: 3g

Easy Fried Spinach

What ingredients you will need:

8 cloves garlic, thinly sliced
2 (10 ounce) bags fresh spinach leaves
1/4 cup unsalted butter
1/4 cup canola oil

Directions:

1) In a skillet melt butter and heat it up along with canola oil. Now add garlic in it and cook until it becomes brown.

2) Finally add spinach in it and cook it for 5 minutes. Make sure that that color of spinach has become dark.

3) Serve and enjoy. This original recipe will give you 6 servings in total.

Nutritional facts per serving:

Serving size: 100g

Calories: 175kcal

Carbohydrates: 20g

Protein: 3g

Fat: 14g

Fiber: 3g

Chinese Soup Recipes

Chinese Lion's Head Soup

What ingredients you will need:

1 pound ground beef
1 tablespoon cornstarch
2 teaspoons sesame oil
1 teaspoon salt
1/4 teaspoon monosodium glutamate (MSG) (optional)
1 tablespoon minced fresh ginger root
2 cups water, or as needed
1 tablespoon soy sauce
2 cups water, or as needed
2 cups low-sodium chicken broth
1 head napa cabbage, cored and cut into chunks
1 tablespoon cornstarch
1 tablespoon vegetable oil
2 green onions, chopped and divided
1 egg
2 green onions, chopped and divided

Directions:

1) Take a bowl and mix together the following ingredients; ground beef, egg, cornstarch, ginger, 2 teaspoons of sesame oil, salt and half chopped green onions.

2) With the help of your hands, toss all the elements well to make sure that they are evenly distributed and set it aside.

3) In a large skillet, heat oil and fry napa cabbage in it. Stir it constantly for 2-3 minutes or until you see the cabbage wilting.

4) Add in the chicken broth, water and soy sauce. Let it boil and then reduce the flame.

5) With the help of spoons, shape the meat mixture into balls.

6) Drop all the balls that you form into the boiling soup mixture and then cover it with a lit. Allow it to cook for 10 minutes.

7) Taste once to adjust salt and sprinkle sesame oil and the leftover green onions for garnishing.

8) Serve and enjoy. This original recipe will give you 4 servings in total.

Nutritional facts per serving:

Serving size: 300g

Calories: 400kcal

Carbohydrates: 7g

Protein: 23g

Fat: 24g

Fiber: 2g

Chinese Sizzling Rice Soup

What ingredients you will need:

2/3 cup uncooked white rice
3 ounces skinless, boneless chicken pieces cut into chunks
3 ounces baby shrimp
1 egg
4 tablespoons cornstarch
4 cups vegetable oil for frying
3 cups chicken broth
1 ounce mushrooms, chopped
1 tablespoon sherry
1/2 teaspoon salt
1/3 cup fresh green beans, cut into 1 inch pieces
1/8 cup diced bamboo shoots
2 tablespoons chopped water chestnuts

Directions:

1) Combine shrimp, chicken, egg and cornstarch.

2)   On the other hand, heat oil in a wok and once it is hot add in shrimp and chicken mixture to it. Cook for 30 seconds and drain it to dispose excessive oil.

3) Take a pot and add in the above mixture along with broth, mushrooms, water chestnuts, bamboo shoots and green beans in it.

4) Allow it to boil and then add sherry and salt. Again allow it to boil and bring the flame to a medium low and let it cook.

5) In the meantime, heat the leftover 1 cup of oil and when it is hot add in rice to it. Brown them quickly and drain them before adding to the soup. Serve hot to enjoy!

6) This original recipe will give you 6 servings in total.

Nutritional facts per serving:

Serving size: 200g

Calories: 300kcal

Carbohydrates: 24g

Protein: 13g

Fat: 14g

Fiber: 1g

Chinese Chicken Soup

What ingredients you will need:

1 quart chicken broth
1 pound chopped cooked chicken breast
2 tablespoons chile paste
2 teaspoons chopped fresh ginger root
1/2 teaspoon ground turmeric
2 tablespoons sesame oil
1/2 cup chopped green onion
1 cup shredded lettuce
1 (3 ounce) package ramen noodles
1 cup chopped celery
1/4 cup soy sauce
2 teaspoons sugar

Directions:

1) Heat up oil in a pot. Now cook turmeric, ginger and chile paste in it for 2 minutes.

2) Add chicken, broth, sugar, soy sauce and celery in it and boil all these ingredients.

3) Finally add noodles in it and cook for 3 minutes.

4) Add lettuce in it and then garnish it with green onion.

5) This original recipe will give you 6 servings in total.

Nutritional facts per serving:

Serving size: 100g

Calories: 165kcal

Carbohydrates: 6g

Protein: 17g

Fat: 8g

Fiber: 1g

Chinese Corn Soup

What ingredients you will need:

1 egg, beaten
1 (14.5 ounce) can low-sodium chicken broth
2 tablespoons water
1 tablespoon cornstarch
1 (15 ounce) can cream style corn

Directions:

1) Mix cream corn and broth in a saucepan and boil both on medium heat.

2) Now mix cornstarch in water and make mixture. Pour this mixture in the boiled soup ingredients and cook it for 3 minutes.

3) Finally add beaten egg in this mixture but continually stir soup while pouring egg in it.

4) Heat through and it is ready to serve.

5) Serve and enjoy. This original recipe will give you 4 servings in total.

Nutritional facts per serving:

Serving size: 100g

Calories: 120kcal

Carbohydrates: 24g

Protein: 5g

Fat: 2g

Fiber: 2g

Chinese Egg Soup

What ingredients you will need:

4 cups seasoned chicken broth
1/2 cup frozen green peas
1 egg, beaten

Directions:

1) Take a large saucepan and mix broth, peas in it. now boil both in the saucepan.

2) Now pour beaten egg in boiled broth but continually stir it.

3) Finally garnish it with any vegetable that you want.

4) Serve and enjoy. This original recipe will give you 6 servings in total.

Nutritional facts per serving:

Serving size: 100g

Calories: 130kcal

Carbohydrates: 10g

Protein: 7g

Fat: 2g

Fiber: 2g

Quick Veggie Soup

What ingredients you will need:

1 (2 pound) package frozen mixed vegetables
1 onion, finely diced
4 potatoes, peeled and cubed
1 (46 fluid ounce) can tomato juice
ground black pepper to taste
2 cups water
4 cubes beef bouillon

Directions:

1) This is one of the easiest Chinese soup recipe. Just take a pot and mix all ingredients in it.

2) Now boil all these ingredients until potatoes are tender. This process usually takes approximately 30 to 40 minutes.

3) Serve and enjoy. This original recipe will give you 6 servings in total.

Nutritional facts per serving:

Serving size: 150g

Calories: 220kcal

Carbohydrates: 40g

Protein: 7g

Fat: 1g
Fiber: 10g

Egg Drop Soup

What ingredients you will need:

2 tablespoons chopped green onion
1 tablespoon cornstarch
1 egg, lightly beaten
2 (14.5 ounce) cans chicken broth

Directions:

1) Take a stockpot and mix broth and cornstarch in it. now boil it on medium heat.

2) Finally pour beaten eggs in the soup and stir continually.

3) Sprinkle chopped green onions in it to garnish it.

4) Soup is ready to serve.

5) Serve and enjoy. This original recipe will give you 4 servings in total.

Nutritional facts per serving:

Serving size: 100g

Calories: 150kcal

Carbohydrates: 10g

Protein: 5g

Fat: 1g

Fiber: 1g

Homemade Wonton Soup

What ingredients you will need:

1/4 teaspoon salt
1/4 cup dry bread crumbs
1 egg
1 tablespoon soy sauce
1 tablespoon sesame oil
1 pound ground beef
6 fresh mushrooms, sliced
1 bunch green onions, cut into 1/2-inch pieces, divided
1 dash sesame oil, to taste (optional)
1 dash soy sauce, or to taste (optional)
16 snow peas
1 medium head bok choy, torn into 2-inch pieces
16 uncooked medium shrimp, peeled and deveined (optional)
8 cups chicken broth
1 (16 ounce) package wonton wrappers
1/2 teaspoon ground black pepper

Directions:

1) Dice green onions and put them sideways. Take out 1 tablespoon from them. Do the same with mushrooms and chop both the 1 tablespoons finely and add in with the ground beef, in a bowl.

2) Add in sesame oil, egg, soy sauce, bread crumbs, salt and pepper. Mix properly!

3) Fill the center of wonton wrappers with the above mentioned filling (1 tablespoon of it). Lightly moisten the edges of wonton wrappers and fold it to make a triangle.

4) Press the edges evenly to seal it and fold in the two edges of the triangle and press hard to close firmly!

5) In a large saucepan, bring chicken broth to boil. Add the wontons one by one in the broth and let them simmer for 3-5 minutes.

6) When they float up to the surface bring the flame to medium low and simmer. Keep stirring gently and add in shrimp, bok choy and the set aside sliced mushrooms.

7) Let the soup cook for another 2 minutes and when the shrimp turns pink; drop them in the snow pea pods.

8) For garnishing use the leftover green onions and a dash of soy sauce and sesame oil. Serve right away!

Nutritional facts per serving:

Serving size: 250g

Calories: 150kcal

Carbohydrates: 40g

Protein: 25g

Fat: 10g

Fiber: 5g

Asian-Style Chicken Noodle Soup

What ingredients you will need:

1/4 cup vinegar
1 pinch cayenne pepper, or to taste
1 pinch ground black pepper, or to taste
1 tablespoon sesame oil
2 teaspoons chopped lemongrass
2 teaspoons minced fresh ginger root
6 stalks celery, diced
6 carrots, diced
1/2 teaspoon onion powder
1/2 teaspoon garlic powder
1/2 teaspoon Chinese five-spice powder
1 teaspoon chicken bouillon
1 teaspoon soy sauce
1 tablespoon shrimp bouillon
4 cups fresh spinach, chopped
1 pound shrimp (31-40 per pound), peeled and deveined
1 tablespoon fish sauce
3 ounces spaghetti
2 bay leaves
1 onion, chopped
1 cup water
1 red bell pepper, chopped
32 ounces chicken broth
Directions:

1) In a stockpot add; chicken stock, bay leaves, water, fish sauce, shrimp bouillon, soy sauce, chicken bouillon, Chinese five-spice powder, garlic powder and onion powder and mix.

2) Bring this mixture to a boil and lower the flame to medium. Put in carrots, celery, red bell pepper and onion.

3) Bring this mixture to a simmer and allow it cook unless the vegetables are soft (for at least 5 minutes).

4) Insert the spaghetti and simmer for 5 minute and bring the flame down to medium low. Further add the following components; shrimp, spinach, vinegar, ginger lemon grass, sesame oil, black pepper and cayenne pepper to it.

5) Stir it and turn the flame off. Let the soup sit for 30 minutes and serve!

6) Serve and enjoy. This original recipe will give you 4 servings in total.

Nutritional facts per serving:

Serving size: 220g

Calories: 320kcal

Carbohydrates: 30g

Protein: 25g

Fat: 5g

Fiber: 8g

Hot and Sour Soup with Tofu

What ingredients you will need:

1/4 teaspoon crushed red pepper flakes
1 (8 ounce) can sliced water chestnuts, drained
1 tablespoon vinegar
1 (8 ounce) package firm tofu, cubed
1 tablespoon soy sauce
6 ounces frozen snow peas
2 cups chicken broth
1 tablespoon sesame oil
2 cups water
3 tablespoons water
3 green onions, chopped
1 tablespoon cornstarch
1 red bell pepper, chopped
1/8 teaspoon ground black pepper
1 tablespoon vegetable oil

Directions:

1) In a large saucepan, heat oil and add in green onions and red bell pepper. Stir fry for 5 minutes.

2) Pour in water, soy sauce and broth and reduce the flame to medium heat. Simmer for another 5 minutes.

3) Take a bowl and combine the following elements; vinegar, red pepper flakes, ground black pepper, cornstarch, 2 tablespoons of water and sesame oil.

4) Pour this mixture into the soup and cook for some time until it starts to thicken.

5) Now mix in the tofu, snow peas and water chestnuts. Let it cook for around 10 minutes and serve hot.

6) Serve and enjoy. This original recipe will give you 4 servings in total.

Nutritional facts per serving:

Serving size: 150g

Calories: 220kcal

Carbohydrates: 15g

Protein: 15g

Fat: 7g

Fiber: 5g

Chinese Salad Recipes

Asian Chicken Salad

What ingredients you will need:

4 boneless chicken breast halves, cooked and shredded
3 tablespoons rice vinegar
1 tablespoon sesame seeds, toasted
3 green onions, chopped
1/4 cup vegetable oil
1 head iceberg lettuce - rinsed, dried, and chopped
1 (8 ounce) package dried rice noodles
1 tablespoon sesame oil (optional)
2 teaspoons soy sauce
2 tablespoons brown sugar

Directions:

1) For the dressing, combine brown sugar, sesame oil, soy sauce, rice vinegar and salad oil. Prepare the dressing 30 minutes before the salad gets ready!

2) Heat skillet and add in oil. For preparing the Chinese rice break the noodles a little and put them in the skillet to fry!

3) They will start puffing as added to the skillet so add only a few at a time. As soon as they start to puff drain them out and add into the salad combination.

4) Take a large bowl and add in iceberg lettuce, cooked and shredded chicken, green onions and toasted sesame seeds.

5) Allow them to chill for at least 10 minutes. Just at the moment of serving add in the rice noodles and serve warm in salad bowls.

6) Serve and enjoy. This original recipe will give you 6 servings in total.

Nutritional facts per serving:

Serving size: 250g

Calories: 400kcal

Carbohydrates: 25g

Protein: 20g

Fat: 10g

Fiber: 2g

Conclusion

Thank you again for downloading this book!

I hope this book was able to help you to create simple and delicious Chinese vegan recipes to enjoy at home.

www.ingramcontent.com/pod-product-compliance
Lightning Source LLC
Chambersburg PA
CBHW071447070526
44578CB00001B/251